Françoise Blanchet and Rinke Doornekamp

What to do with . . . a potato

Barron's/Woodbury

All inquiries should be addressed to:
Barron's Educational Series, Inc.
113 Crossways Park Drive
Woodbury, New York 11797

Library of Congress Catalog Card No. 77-85383

International Standard Book No. 0-8120-5255-2

PRINTED IN THE NETHERLANDS

Foreword

This book, first published in Holland, is the work of a French woman, Françoise Blanchet. Ms. Blanchet's parents run a well-known restaurant in Paris, and she herself studied at the Hotel School in Lausanne. When Ms. Blanchet married and moved to Holland, she had the idea of writing cookbooks for children. She worked closely with this book's illustrator, Rinke Doornekamp, trying to make the recipes and illustrations as clear and entertaining as possible. We think you'll agree that Ms. Blanchet has done just that in this fun-filled collection of recipes.

Philip and Mary Hyman

Contents

Boiled potatoes

1 Peel potatoes and put into pot. Fill pot with cold water and add a pinch of salt. Bring water to a boil and cook for 20 minutes.
2 Prick potatoes with a fork. If they are soft, they are done.
3 Pour off water (hold potatoes inside pot with the cover!). Delicious served hot with butter, salt, and pepper.

Hint: make a lot of potatoes. Cooked, they can be used in many recipes.

Ham and potato salad

Ingredients (for 1): 1 tablespoon vinegar; 3 tablespoons oil; salt; pepper; 2 cold boiled potatoes; 2 small pickles; 1 slice ham; 1 lettuce leaf; 1 hard-boiled egg; 1 sprig parsley.

Put the vinegar, oil, salt, and pepper into a bowl and stir with a fork to make the salad dressing.

Cut the potatoes, pickles, and ham into little pieces, then stir them gently into the dressing. Cover the bottom of a small salad bowl with a leaf of lettuce. Pour in the salad with all its dressing. Put sliced hard-boiled egg around the salad and a sprig of parsley on top to decorate.

Fisherman's potato salad

Ingredients (for 1): 2 cold boiled potatoes; 1 tomato; 1/2 cup cooked shrimp, crab, or fish; 2 tablespoons mayonnaise; salt; pepper; 1 lettuce leaf; 1 teaspoon ketchup; 1 sprig parsley.

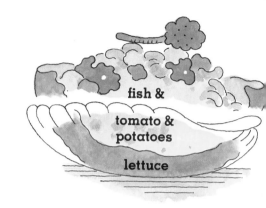

fish &

tomato & potatoes

lettuce

Cut potatoes and tomatoes into little pieces. Place in a bowl with shrimp, crab, or fish, the mayonnaise, salt, and pepper. Gently mix with a spoon to make the salad.

Put the lettuce leaf on the bottom of a small salad bowl (or on the bottom of a large sea shell if you have one!). Cover leaf with potato salad. Decorate top of salad with a spoonful of ketchup and a sprig of parsley.

Mashed potatoes

Ingredients (for 1): 3 peeled potatoes; 2 tablespoons butter; 1/2 cup milk; salt; pepper; and a pinch of nutmeg.

Boil potatoes, then pour off water. While still hot, mash potatoes until smooth. Then stir in butter, milk, a little salt and pepper, and a pinch of nutmeg. Put mashed potatoes back on the stove to reheat. Serve very hot, but don't let them dry out—mashed potatoes should be thick and creamy.

Delicious with sausages or liver!

Croquettes

Ingredients (for 1): 1 egg; 3 heaping tablespoons cold mashed potatoes; breadcrumbs; 3 tablespoons butter.

1 Break egg into a cup and beat with a fork.
2 Dip spoonfuls of the cold mashed potatoes into beaten egg.
3 Roll each mashed potato ball in breadcrumbs.
4 Heat the butter in a frying pan. Add potato croquettes. Brown carefully on both sides (don't cook too many at a time) using two forks to turn them over. Serve very hot.

Fried sliced potatoes

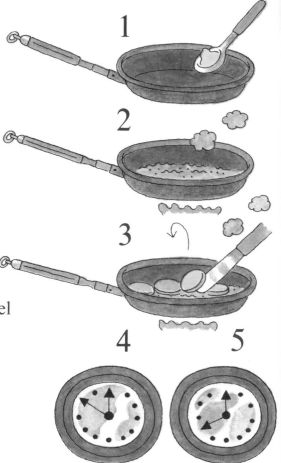

1 Put some butter into a frying pan.
2 Heat the butter until it just begins to
   brown.
3 Slice some potatoes and fry them in the
   butter (be sure to turn them over so they
   brown on both sides). Sprinkle with salt
   and pepper. Serve hot.

Hint:
4 Sliced boiled potatoes fry in 10 minutes.
5 Sliced raw potatoes fry in 20 minutes (peel
   raw potatoes before cooking them).

Potato pancakes

1. slice the cold potatoes
2. cut the slices into strips
3. heat 2 tablespoons of butter in a pan
4. add all the potatoes at once
5. spread out evenly
6. press together with a fork

Ingredients (for 1): 3 cold boiled potatoes; 4 tablespoons butter (or oil).

7

after 5 min. slide onto a plate

8

cover with a second plate

9

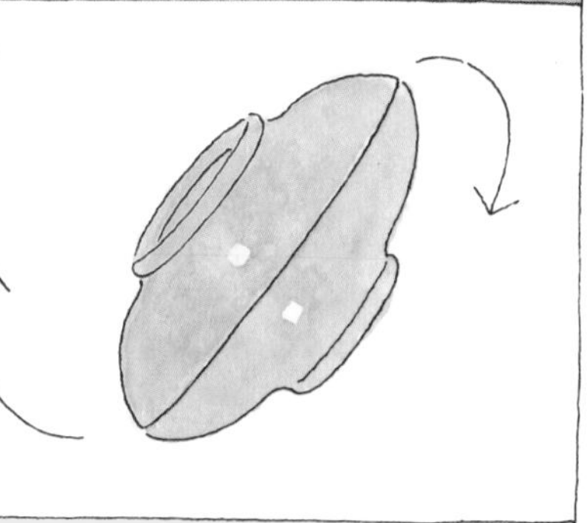

turn upside down

10

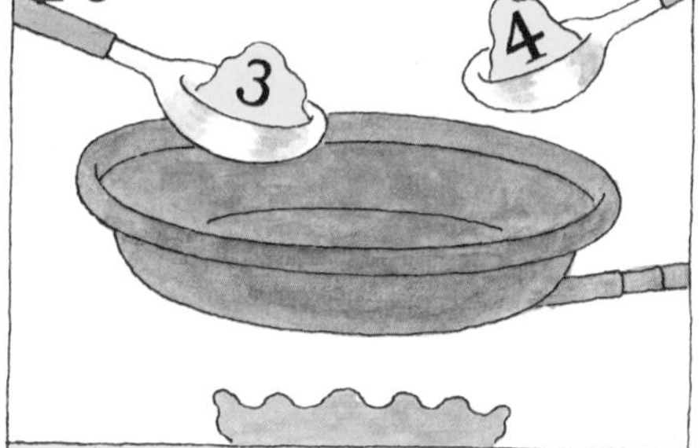

add rest of butter to pan

11

cook 5 min. more

12

try with chicken and salad

Potato balls

Ingredients (for 1): 4 large potatoes; 3 tablespoons butter; salt; pepper; chopped parsley.

Peel potatoes. Use a scooper to make perfect little potato balls. Scoop out as many balls from each potato as possible.

Heat butter in a frying pan. Add potato balls and shake pan often so they don't stick! Add salt and pepper. Cook until balls are golden brown outside and soft inside—taste one (careful, they're hot!). Sprinkle with parsley and serve.

Hint: after scooping out the potato balls, save the rest of the potatoes. Put them in a bowl of cold water in the refrigerator. They can be used later to make mashed potatoes.

Hashed brown potatoes

Ingredients (for 1): 3 potatoes (peeled); 3 tablespoons butter; salt; pepper; chopped parsley.

Cut potatoes into thick slices (watch your fingers!).

Cut slices into strips, then strips into cubes (see pictures 1, 2, and 3).

1   2   3

Heat butter in frying pan. Add cubes and a little salt and pepper. Stir occasionally. Cook until golden brown. Sprinkle with chopped parsley and serve hot.

Hint: little pieces of bacon can be fried with the potatoes and some fresh chives can be chopped with the parsley. Delicious!

Baking potatoes

General comments:
Be careful when using the oven. Always wear special pot-holder gloves—baking dishes get very hot!

Have a baking sheet and oven-proof dish ready before starting.

Turn oven on 15 minutes before you put anything in to bake.

These baked dishes can be a whole meal!

Meat and potato casserole

1

Mash potatoes as explained

2

mix meat with herbs and spices

3

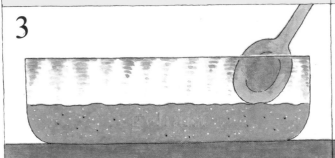

place meat in the baking dish

4

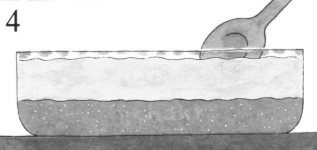

cover with mashed potatoes

Ingredients (for 1): mashed potatoes (3 potatoes); 1/2 cup ground meat; chopped herbs and garlic; salt; pepper; 3 pats butter.

5

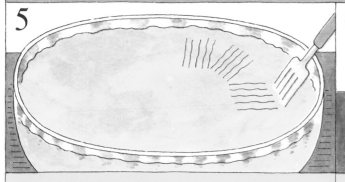

decorate surface with a fork

6

dot with pats of butter

7

bake for 45 minutes in a 425°F oven

8

delicious served with a salad!

Ham and potato casserole

Ingredients (for 1): 10 small potatoes; 2 tablespoons butter; 2 tomatoes; 1/2 cup diced ham; chopped parsley; salt; pepper; 1 bouillon cube; 1/2 cup hot water.

Wash potatoes but don't peel. Butter a baking dish. Cut potatoes in half and put into baking dish. Cut tomatoes into small pieces. Put tomatoes, ham, and parsley into baking dish with potatoes. Sprinkle with salt and pepper.

Dissolve bouillon cube in hot water, then pour into baking dish. Sprinkle everything with breadcrumbs.

Bake in a 425°F oven for one hour, then serve.

Winter dinner

Ingredients (for 1): 3 large peeled potatoes; 5 slices cheese; 1 egg; 1/2 cup milk; salt; pepper; nutmeg; 3 pats butter.

Cut potatoes into thin slices. Lightly butter a baking dish and cover bottom with some potato slices. Place a slice of cheese on top of potatoes, then continue making layers of potatoes, cheese, potatoes, cheese, until the dish is almost full (make the top layer of cheese!).

Beat egg and milk together and season with salt, pepper, and nutmeg, then pour over potatoes and cheese. Place three pats of butter on top. Bake in a 400°F oven for one hour. Serve hot.

Stuffed baked potatoes

Ingredients (for 1): 1 large potato; 1 slice
salami or other sausage; 2 hard-boiled eggs; 4
fresh mushrooms; 1 sprig parsley; salt; pepper;
1 pat butter; 2 slices cheese.

1 Wash the potato (don't peel it!).
2 Bake 45 minutes in a 425°F oven.
3 Cut sausage, eggs, mushrooms, and parsley into
   little pieces. Mix in a bowl with salt and pepper.
4 Cut the hot potato in half (careful!).
5 Scoop out the inside (don't break the skin!).
6 Mix potato pulp with other ingredients.
7 Fill each half-potato skin with half the stuffing.
   Dot the top with a little butter.
8 Place a slice of cheese on each half-potato.
   Put back in the oven for another 15 minutes.
   Serve when the cheese has melted.

Silver potatoes with cream

1 — wash the potatoes

2 — wrap in aluminum foil

3 — bake 1 hour in a 425°F oven

4 — cut the ham into cubes

5 — place the cubes in a bowl

6 — add cream and milk to ham

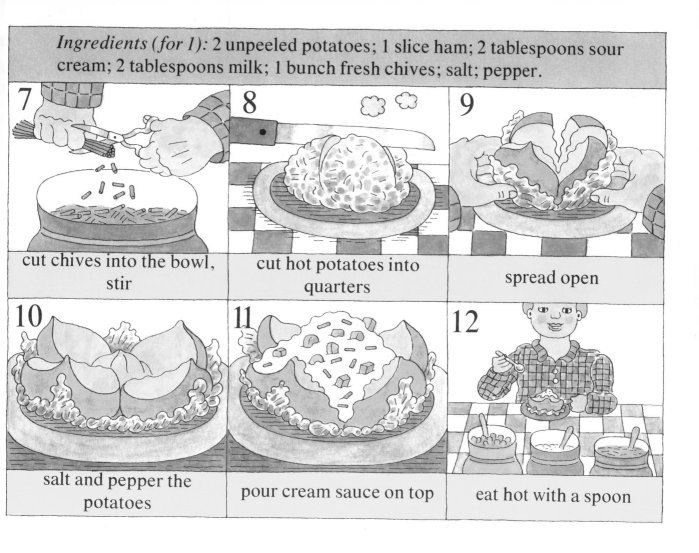

Ingredients (for 1): 2 unpeeled potatoes; 1 slice ham; 2 tablespoons sour cream; 2 tablespoons milk; 1 bunch fresh chives; salt; pepper.

7 cut chives into the bowl, stir

8 cut hot potatoes into quarters

9 spread open

10 salt and pepper the potatoes

11 pour cream sauce on top

12 eat hot with a spoon

French fries

Be careful! Ask your mother to help you make these. Hot fat is dangerous.

1 Peel the potatoes.
2 Cut into thin slices, then into strips.
3 Wash the slices.
4 Pat them dry with a towel.
5 Cook in a special deep-frying pot.
6 Drain potatoes on a paper towel.
7 Serve hot with salt.

Potatoes can be cut into any shape you like before frying. The smaller the slices, the faster they cook. Don't cook too many at one time.

Different fried potatoes

Hint: All deep-fried potatoes must cook in very hot fat or oil. Drop a test potato piece in—if it sizzles immediately, add the others. If not, wait, then try again. Be careful not to let the hot fat splatter!

Potato chips: use a potato slicer to slice the potatoes very thin. Cook like French fries, described earlier.

Potato wafers: cut this design with a special slicer. Cook just like French fries.

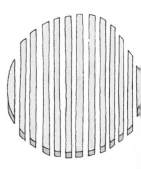

Match sticks: slice the potatoes, then cut each slice into very thin strips. Cook like French fries.

Twice-fried potatoes

These are complicated.
Cut the potatoes into thicker slices than for French fries. Cut the slices into strips. Deep-fry them for three or four minutes, but don't let them color. Remove and drain. Heat the fat until it is hotter than before (but *don't* let it smoke). Cook the potatoes again until golden brown. Drain and serve.

Thick double fries: these are very thick (about 1/2 inch). Cook as described above.

Diced double fries: cut the thick slices into cubes. Cook as described above.

Hint: leftover pieces of peeled raw potatoes can be put in cold water and saved in the refrigerator to make mashed potatoes another day.

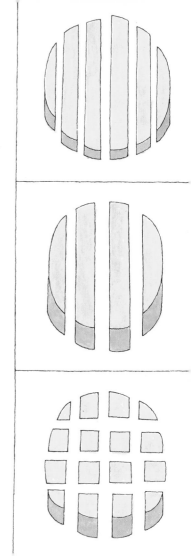

Rules to follow when cooking

1 Always wash your hands before cooking.
2 Wear an apron.
3 Be careful when deep-frying potatoes. If the fat smokes, lower the heat. If it catches on fire, cover the pot—*Don't Add Water!* Ask your mother's help when deep-frying.